TRACK DOWN THE SNEAKY HACKERS WITH ...

# SCIENTISTS in ACTION!

# Cyber Spy Hunters!

# SCIENTISTS in ACTION!

Archaeologists!

Astronauts!

Big-Animal Vets!

Biomedical Engineers!

Civil Engineers!

Climatologists!

Crime Scene Techs!

Cyber Spy Hunters!

Marine Biologists!

Robot Builders!

# SCIENTISTS in ACTION!

# Cyber Spy Hunters!

### By Mari Rich

**Mason Crest**
450 Parkway Drive, Suite D
Broomall, PA 19008
www.masoncrest.com

Printed and bound in the United States of America.

Series ISBN: 978-1-4222-3416-7
Hardback ISBN: 1-4222-3424-2
EBook ISBN: 1-4222-8485-8

First printing
1 3 5 7 9 8 6 4 2

Produced by Shoreline Publishing Group LLC
Santa Barbara, California
Editorial Director: James Buckley Jr.
Designer: Tom Carling, Carling Design Inc.
Production: Sandy Gordon
www.shorelinepublishing.com

Cover image: Lockheed Martin Corporation

Library of Congress Cataloging-in-Publication Data
Rich, Mari, author.
        Cyber spy hunters! / by Mari Rich.
        pages cm. -- (Scientists in action!)
        Audience: Grades 9 to 12
Includes bibliographical references and index.
ISBN 978-1-4222-3424-2 (hardback : alk. paper) -- ISBN 978-1-4222-3416-7 (series : alk. paper) -- ISBN 978-1-
4222-8485-8 (ebook) 1. Computer crimes--Investigation--Juvenile literature. 2. Computer security--Juvenile
literature. 3. Hackers--Juvenile literature. I. Title.
HV8079.C65R53 2016
363.25'968--dc23
                                2015004676

# Contents

## Key Icons to Look For

**Words to Understand:** These words with their easy-to-understand definitions will increase the reader's understanding of the text, while building vocabulary skills.

**Sidebars:** This boxed material within the main text allows readers to build knowledge, gain insights, explore possibilities, and broaden their perspectives by weaving together additional information to provide realistic and holistic perspectives.

**Research Projects:** Readers are pointed toward areas of further inquiry connected to each chapter. Suggestions are provided for projects that encourage deeper research and analysis.

**Text-Dependent Questions:** These questions send the reader back to the text for more careful attention to the evidence presented here.

**Series Glossary of Key Terms:** This back-of-the-book glossary contains terminology used throughout this series. Words found here increase the reader's ability to read and comprehend higher-level books and articles in this field.

# Action!

*I*t was almost a disaster. From the outside, there was very little indication that one of the worst **breaches** of U.S. military computers in history was occurring. A troubling signal, though, began coming from within the secure network that housed the country's most important secrets. Among those secrets were highly **classified** battle plans for operations in Iraq and Afghanistan.

## WORDS TO UNDERSTAND

**breaches**  breaks in a wall, barrier, or defense

**classified**  kept secret from all but a few people in the government or an organization

**malware**  a software program designed to damage or perform unwanted actions on a computer system

**nefarious**  wicked or criminal

**propaganda**  the organized spread of certain ideas to help a political cause or government

**thumb drive**  a small electronic device, also known as a **flash drive,** used for storing data or transferring it to and from a computer, digital camera, or other device

A crack team of cyber experts was summoned to a windowless, computer-filled room in Ops-1. This ordinary-looking building near Washington, D.C., is the home of the National Security Agency (NSA). It is the government organization responsible for safeguarding national security information systems, including those used by the Department of Defense.

There in Ops-1, the team discovered a spy, but it wasn't a human one. It was, instead, a piece of **malware**—a computer program that was trying to send coded messages back to whoever had created it.

The U.S. military's computer system reportedly includes more than 15,000 networks and seven million computers in hundreds of facilities around the globe. Almost 100,000 people are employed to keep it running. While that gives the United States important advantages over our enemies, there is also the possibility that those enemies can use our technology against us. They mount cyber attacks—assaults on our computer systems and networks. They could steal important research data and spy on sensitive communications. They could copy designs for weapons, or disrupt military maneuvers. They could alter data so that authorized users make decisions based on wrong information, and they could send misleading information into America as **propaganda**.

Cyber attackers try to do this **nefarious** activity anonymously. They hide their identity by routing their attacks through countries that are unfriendly to us or by taking over computer servers in neutral countries. They also can do it inexpensively. Cyber attacks don't require massive aircraft carriers or high-tech stealth jets. A cyber spy can operate from anywhere.

The NSA has the world's largest array of supercomputers, along with a factory for making its own computer chips. It also employs some of the world's brightest, most technologically adept people. As soon as that troubling signal was discovered in 2008 by an NSA monitor, the nation's top cyber spy hunters got to work. They learned that the malware had been analyzed a few months earlier by a computer expert in Finland, who had dubbed it "Agent.btz." The attack had infected the Secret Internet Protocol Router Network, which the Department of Defense uses to transmit classified information. It was also inside the Joint Worldwide Intelligence Communication System, which sends super-secret material to U.S. officials wherever they are stationed throughout the world.

Soldiers often work with computers, gathering data, writing reports, and communicating with people back home or in the field. In 2008, hackers used that access to attack military computers.

Those networks were "air-gapped." That means they were separated physically and electronically from other networks that might be unsecured. Somehow, however, Agent.btz had gotten in anyway. NSA cyber spy hunters couldn't tell right away who had created the malware, but they had their suspicions. Russia's Foreign Intelligence Service was at the top of the list. The NSA also didn't know how long Agent.btz had been lurking on the U.S. system. Those were important questions, but it was even more important to neutralize the malware as quickly as possible and stop it from spreading.

The team members worked throughout the night, fortifying themselves with pizza and soft drinks. By morning, they had come up with computer code that ordered Agent.btz to shut itself down. That was only the first step, however. Now they had to track down Agent.btz everywhere it had spread on government networks. That turned into

The ability of a thumb drive to contain enormous amounts of information is a relatively new development. The portability of viruses and malware makes them much harder to attack and track.

## What Is a Hacker?

When most people think of hackers, they think of bad guys who try to break into computer systems to steal, spy, or do all sorts of harm. Others say a hacker is anyone who is very good at computer programming and who can find out where the problems are in a piece of computer code and fix them. These people say hacking is a very important skill that could be compared to knowing how to operate a bulldozer, for example. Sure, you could go around using your bulldozer to knock down buildings just to be destructive. Or you could use that same bulldozer for better purposes, such as helping construct new buildings. Today, many people use the term "black-hat hacker" to mean anyone who uses their programming skills to steal or spy. The term "white-hat hacker" refers to someone who uses their skills for good, such as helping to keep systems safe.

a long-term task that involved taking individual computers off the networks, cleaning them up, and reformatting their hard drives.

Now that the immediate danger had passed, agents asked another question: How had the malware infected their networks? The answer to that big problem turned out to be only the size of a thumb. The team believed that a soldier or military contractor stationed in the Middle East had, without knowing it, used his **thumb drive** to infect the system. He had copied it from an infected computer at an Internet café. Then the malware had spread when his drive was put into his military laptop.

As hard as they tried, agents could not discover the specific thumb drive that started the problem. If they had, its owner would have been in big trouble. Probably without meaning to, he or she had collaborated with Agent.btz, one of the most dangerous spies in military history.

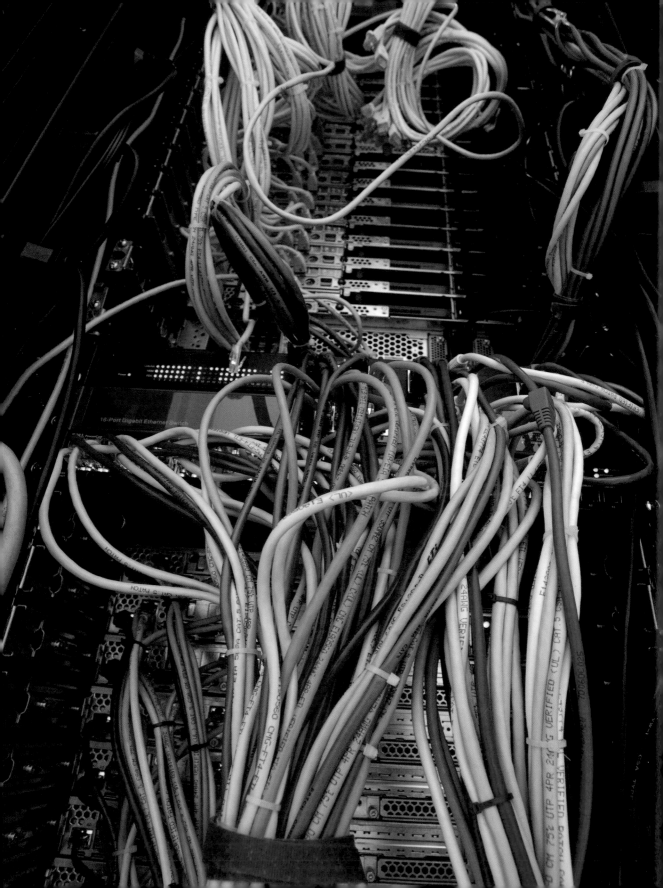

# The Scientists and Their Science

Every part of life in the United States relies heavily on computers. That includes banking, transportation, **telecommunications**, and medical care. So it's not just the military that is at great risk for a cyber attack. Black-hat hackers could use their programming skills to

## WORDS TO UNDERSTAND

**elite**   the part or group having the highest quality or importance

**epilepsy**   a medical condition marked by abnormal electrical discharges in the brain

**predator**   a person that stalks other people, or an animal that stalks other animals

**telecommunications**   communication between people far away from each other using telephone, email, or computer

**viruses**   hidden computer programs that produce copies of themselves, insert them into other programs, and usually perform malicious actions, such as destroying data; also known as worms or Trojan horses

FEDERAL BUREAU OF INVESTIGATION

The FBI and other government agencies actively recruit future cyber security experts to work for them, in hopes of staying ahead of the black-hat hackers.

steal credit card information or social-security numbers. They could disrupt power and water supplies, get industry secrets from a business competitor, or totally shut down a network. In addition, if you don't think a hacker can actually hurt someone physically, think again! In 2008, a Web site for people who suffer from **epilepsy** was hacked by vandals. They programmed the site to flash bright images rapidly. Epileptic seizures can sometimes be triggered by flashing lights, so that was a foolish and dangerous prank.

Some experts say that every second of the day, *nine* new pieces of malware are developed! Large U.S. companies spend more than $12 million per year each combating and defending against cyber attacks. It's easy to understand why there is such a need to keep cyberspace safe and secure. The experts who do that work are basically cyber spy hunters.

# Agents at Work

*I*n addition to the NSA, there are many government agencies that hire cyber security experts. The Federal Bureau of Investigation (FBI) maintains many cyber units, including **elite**, highly trained Cyber Action Teams (CATs). Like a military strike team, they travel the world responding to cyber threats.

If you watch the news, you've probably seen Secret Service agents wearing sunglasses and earpieces protecting the president or other dignitaries. Sometimes people send threats to the president by email. The Secret Service has cyber agents who investigate each threat. They might even visit the writer in the field to see if the threat is serious. Cyber agents also travel ahead of the president and other government leaders when they have appointments outside of the White House. These agents make sure that any computerized systems, such as those that run the elevators and air conditioners in the big buildings they enter, have not been hacked.

Not all cyber security experts work for government organizations. You probably have software on your computer that protects it from **viruses**. The companies that make that software, such as Kaspersky Labs and McAfee, employ hundreds of experts. They design, build, test, and update the protection software you buy. Social media sites such as Twitter and Facebook also need cyber security experts. That's to make sure no one is misusing or hacking into their sites. Businesses, from banks to stores to manufacturers, have their own cyber security forces, too.

Many people who work as cyber security experts say they love their jobs because their days are so varied and interesting. FBI Special Agent Brian T. Herrick says, "In my computer forensic work alone, on any given day I might be examining the logs of a network intrusion, interviewing an Internet fraud victim, analyzing the seized computer of a child **predator**, or doing research for a cyber terrorism case. For example, helping the bank-robbery squad retrieve some digital images of a recent holdup from a bank surveillance camera." Herrick's team can find out how the thieves hacked into the video system to get those pictures.

# Cyber Security Skills

You may be wondering if you have what it takes for a career in cyber security. It's not enough to be good at science and math, although that helps. Candace Worley is a senior vice president and general manager of endpoint security at the Intel Security Group. She says that a job at a big company like hers, or at a government agency such as the NSA might be for you if you are . . .

**Someone Who Thrives on Excitement:** When there is a threat, you must swing into action! Your pulse will race and your mind will be totally focused on the task at hand. It doesn't matter whether it's the middle of the night or the weekend. Security breaches can happen at any time.

**A Warrior:** Cyber security experts aren't just people with jobs—they're people on a mission. They are passionate about thwarting the bad guys, and if you don't have that passion, too, you'll probably want to consider a different career.

**An Innovator:** Technology is always evolving. The bad guys keep finding new ways to mount cyber attacks, so the good guys have to be just as clever in thinking up new ways to stop them. It's a constant learning environment.

Cyber security experts spend a lot of time in front of screens. Active investigations, though, can be fast-paced, with seconds sometimes meaning the difference between success and failure.

**A Sleuth:** Do you like detective stories? If you're observant, quick-witted, and good at solving puzzles, you could be a cyber security expert.

**A Tinkerer:** Do you like taking apart things to understand how they work? Dissecting hardware and software to uncover security flaws before an attacker does is one of the most important parts of keeping the world secure. If you're up to solving this technically intense challenge, a cyber security career may be for you.

**A Teacher:** Many people don't understand what they should be doing to protect themselves when using a computer, a smartphone, or the Internet. As a cyber security expert, you can help them learn.

**A Caretaker:** This one might surprise you, but it's true! When you work in cyber security, you are basically protecting people. You're almost like a police officer or firefighter, except that you are protecting

Helping young people understand the importance of computer security is a big part of the work of cyber security experts. Learning how to protect data early makes it a lifelong habit.

millions and millions of people at a time. You'll be keeping thieves from gaining access to people's bank accounts, making sure kids don't reveal too much personal information online, and stopping cyberbullies in their tracks. Many cyber security experts—even the really tough guys—say that this is their favorite part of the job!

## Getting Started

*I*f you're a young person who wants to learn to be a white-hat hacker, you can attend the annual r00tz conference. This event, held in connection with DEF CON, is a popular gathering for tech-savvy adults. The organizers of r00tz say the Internet is a small place,

At DEFCON, groups of professional computer experts sometimes take part in hacking games, designed to practice uncovering attacks on systems that might later translate into real-life situations.

and that kid hackers must follow certain rules. Those rules include hacking only things they already own, respecting the rights of others, and knowing the law. Hacking gives you great power, they say, and it's your responsibility to use that power for good!

Later, you might want to take part in one of the many cyber security competitions held around the country each year. The biggest cyber security contest for students in the world takes place during Cyber Security Awareness Week and includes more than 20,000 students. High school students can compete in a contest that asks them to solve a murder mystery or other criminal case by examining a series of digital clues, such as cell phone records and Web browsing history. Students pit their technology skills against teams from some of the top high schools in the country. They gather each year in Brooklyn, New York, to solve the mystery, meet other young computer experts, and even talk to representatives from technology companies where they may want to work one day.

 **Text-Dependent Questions**

1. How many new pieces of malware do experts estimate are developed every second?

2. What does the Secret Service do when someone emails a threat to the president?

3. Can you name two places that hire cyber security experts?

 **Research Project**

Go online and see where and when DEF CON and r00tz will next be taking place. Make a list of the questions you would ask the experts there if you got to attend.

# Tools of the Trade

2

Law-enforcement officials sometimes refer to "the smoking gun," meaning obvious evidence that proves without a doubt how the crime was committed; imagine a police officer walking into a murder scene and seeing a recently fired gun on the floor and you'll realize where the expression originated. However, dealing with digital evidence—any information or data stored on, or transmitted by, an electronic device—isn't so simple. For one thing, it's usually not in plain sight; the human eye can't see the electrical pulses that transfer or store computer

## WORDS TO UNDERSTAND

**firewalls**   systems designed to prevent unauthorized access to or from a private computer network

**latent**   present, but not visible

**metadata**   tells how, when, and by whom a particular set of data is collected, as well as how the data is formatted

data! As with other **latent** evidence such as fingerprints or DNA, it takes special skills and equipment to analyze it. It is also easily damaged or destroyed if not handled properly, meaning that only highly trained agents or technicians should attempt to work with it.

Cyber criminals can make an investigator's work very hard. They can use software to break a file into parts and hide them within the system, disguise a file so it looks like something harmless or unimportant, or change the date the file was first created and last accessed. They also can be sneaky enough to avoid using devices such as laptops or smartphones; some criminals have discovered that even handheld video games can be used to store, view, and share illegal information. A savvy investigator is aware of all those tricks and is persistent in finding the evidence needed to make the case.

One of the good things about being a cyber security expert: You can work just about anywhere.

# Securing the Evidence

*T*he first thing any good investigator does is to secure the evidence. Just as it's easy to smudge a fingerprint if you don't know it's there, digital evidence can be contaminated. To avoid this, investigators first make a copy of everything on the storage device, whether that is a computer's hard drive, a disk, or a tiny flash drive. They use their own storage devices, which are either brand new or meticulously wiped clean in a forensically proper way in order to avoid contaminating the evidence with old material. (Imagine if an investigator used a disc that already contained evidence from a previous case; the two cases could become confused, and the evidence would not be useful in court.) Agents must keep track of the evidence's chain of custody, so they carefully document how the evidence is handled every step of the way, from the moment it's first discovered to the time it's presented to a judge.

Investigators use devices called write blockers, which allow them to read information from a drive without accidentally damaging the contents. They do this by allowing "read commands" to pass through the system, but by blocking "write commands." Information can be viewed but not added to, deleted, or changed in any other way. They then make a bit-by-bit copy of the data for preservation and analysis.

To prove that none of the evidence has been altered, digital forensic scientists can verify "hashes," which are strings of letters and numbers associated with pieces of data, such as files or images. Just like no two people share the same exact fingerprint, even when they look alike, no two pieces of unique data—no matter how similar they look—can have the same hash.

# Analyzing the Evidence

Cyber security experts can detect many things once they start to analyze what they have gathered. One major piece of evidence can be the IP (Internet Protocol) address, which is a unique string of numbers assigned to every computer on a network. In the same way that your physical mailing address lets the U.S. Postal Service get your letters and bills to you, an IP address allows your computer to send and receive information. (Sometimes, however, a knowledgeable criminal will send communications through a series of other computers with different IP addresses, covering his tracks, so investigators can't always use this information to successfully identify or track the culprit.)

Cyber agents will look at all the files they have copied and can even restore files that have been hidden or deleted, using special software. Sometimes they use a technique called file carving, which allows them to recover files and fragments of files when important **metadata** is corrupt or missing. When U.S. Navy SEALs found hard disks and removable storage devices during a raid of terrorist Osama Bin Laden's compound, computer experts used file carving to find out every bit of information on them.

Besides looking at a suspect's hardware, forensic analysts can trace the Web sites suspects have visited, look at chat rooms they have participated in, view their emails and instant messages, examine online purchases they have made, and more. This can help build a timeline of the criminal activity.

# More Than Just Digital

Some security experts don't believe that it's good enough to detect malicious attacks only after they get past traditional cyber defenses, like antivirus protection and **firewalls**. They use "honey pots" or "honey nets"—software meant to lure black-hat hackers into thinking a system is vulnerable, and then nabbing them. One expert, Eric Winsborrow, calls his traps "shadow networks" and says that

After the cyber security workers have located the source of the attacks, direct action by armed investigators is sometimes called for. Cyber attacks can cause great harm and need a strong response.

when bad guys enter the shadow network, they can be fooled into revealing themselves. Security experts can then observe their methods, discover their true intentions, and plan effective countermeasures. Winsborrow explains that while secret agents often use various technologies, his technology actually is the secret agent.

Special Agent Jim Cole works for Homeland Security Investigations, and he specializes in helping find children who are being abused or exploited. His job requires analyzing countless digital images, and while he has the most sophisticated software and equipment at his disposal, sometimes, he says, there is just no substitute for the human eye.

## Steganography

Sometimes agents have to use special software to decode the data they find. That's because criminals use a technique called steganography, which allows them to encode or hide illicit information within innocent-looking images on public Web sites. In one case, the FBI found that foreign spies were transmitting detailed maps of American airports that way.

Historians say the process dates to the fifth century BCE, when a Greek ruler shaved a servant's hair, tattooed a message on his head about a planned military attack, and waited for the hair to grow back before sending him out to deliver the information to military commanders.

In one case, he spotted a highway sign in the background of a picture of an exploited child.

"We drove every highway in the state of Kansas that ran east to west and started with the number two," Cole says, explaining how agents found and rescued the child.

Another time, a victim was photographed fishing outdoors with her abuser. Cole and his fellow agents consulted with scientists, who studied the trees and fish in the picture and helped them narrow down the location to Minnesota. When they showed the background of the photo to people who worked in the parks and recreation industry there, they were able to pinpoint the exact location where the crime had occurred—information that resulted in her rescue.

Other useful clues that turn up in pictures include logos on clothing, identifiable cars, and building numbers. Once, agents viewed a disturbing video of a child being abused and noticed a bag of pretzels visible in one frame. Because the brand of pretzels was sold only in a certain region, the sharp-eyed agents had gained a valuable clue!

# Text-Dependent Questions

1. Why does data have to be secured before being analyzed?
2. Can deleted files ever be restored by cyber experts?
3. What is steganography?

# Research Project

Cryptography is different from steganography, because an encrypted message (one that has been changed using a cryptographic method) is out in plain sight—it just needs to be deciphered. Cryptography has been used for thousands of years; the ancient Romans used a system called the Caesar cipher. Go online to find out more about the Caesar cipher and how it worked. Can you find other examples of cryptography being used throughout history?

## WORDS TO UNDERSTAND

**fraudulent** done to trick someone

**inappropriate** not proper or fitting

**lingo** the special language used for a particular activity or by a particular group of people

**masterminds** people who supply the direction or creative intelligence for a project

**phishing** creating a false Web site or online identity in order to steal information

**rig** manipulate or control, usually by dishonest means

**vulnerability** capable of being attacked or damaged

# Tales From the Field!

Almost every day, reports of a cyber attack hit the news sites and newspapers. Usually, they include information about how cyber security experts found the hacks and disabled them. Many people often have to change passwords or software following such attacks. In some cases, it can take months to recover data or money. However, in many cases, you will never hear about the work of cyber security experts. They have succeeded when the attack is stopped, not when it makes news. They have worked behind the scenes to make sure the black hats don't get their way.

Here are some cases that show some of the ways that cyber security experts work . . . and some of the threats they face down.

## The Rigged Election

Everyone knows that the job of president in a student government is an important one, but most people don't want it badly enough to cheat. Matthew Weaver, who was attending California State University–San Marcos in 2012, apparently did want the job that badly. He set out to **rig** the election using his knowledge of computers. Weaver bought 15 keyloggers, which are devices that can secretly record what a person is

With the growth of electronic voting, government officials need to be even more careful than ever to prevent voter fraud by black-hat hackers.

typing when online. He installed them on public computers around his campus. The keyloggers recorded everything tapped out on the computer keyboard—including his fellow students' login names, passwords, and email. Weaver quickly gathered information from more than 700 people. On Election Day, he used their identities to vote for himself online.

School officials were monitoring the election, however, and noticed that hundreds of votes were coming from a single laptop computer. They traced the IP address—the unique string of numbers that can single out a particular networked device—and sent a police officer to the building. They found Weaver hunched over his laptop, casting his **fraudulent** ballots. Although he tried to lie and tell the officer he was only doing a school assignment, he was promptly arrested.

The FBI did not let Weaver's identity theft and wire fraud go unpunished. Cyber agents examined Weaver's computer and found a chart he had made, listing each of his victims and the information he had stolen from them. He was prosecuted by the federal government and sent to prison for a year.

# Way Worse Than a Rotten Review

In late 2014, employees of Sony Pictures got to their desks and booted up their computers. Instead of a friendly welcome, they were greeted by a frightening sight: creepy images of human skeletons and misspelled warnings that their system had been hacked. The warnings said that secret internal data had been stolen, and they made threats of further damage.

Things got worse quickly. Cyber security agents jumped to work and found that the hackers had stolen completed films, movie scripts, internal memos, and personal information about actors and Sony employees. Sony officials immediately ordered everyone to stop using their computers. The workers got out paper and pens and tried to keep working.

Security experts quickly discovered a piece of malware called Destover, which had been written in Korean. That provided a good clue as to the nationality of the culprits, since most malware is written in English or Russian. Another clue: It was strikingly similar to malware called DarkSeoul, which had been used previously by North Korean spies to hack into their enemies' systems.

Many observers now strongly believe that the North Korean government was responsible. They point to the fact that when the breach happened, Sony was getting ready to release a comedy film called *The Interview*. The plot involved a plan to kill North Korean leader Kim Jong-un. North Korean officials had publicly condemned the film, saying, "Those who defamed our supreme leadership . . . can never escape the stern punishment to be meted out." That stern punishment just might have been a serious and costly hack. However, while the U.S. government believed North Korea was behind the attack, some computer security experts disagreed. They pointed to former Sony employees or a different outside group as the culprits. The controversy just shows how hard it is to track down cyber criminals.

# A Bad Impersonation

Christopher Patrick Gunn had little in common with Justin Bieber. For one thing, Gunn was 31 years old in 2012—far from a teenager. Gunn, however, pretended to be the popular singer online and ended up tricking hundreds of girls. His scam worked like this: Through Internet-based video chat services, Gunn contacted girls from the ages of about 9 to 16. He claimed to be the star. He then offered to send free concert tickets, backstage passes, or fan merchandise. All the girls had to do in exchange was to send him Web cam videos or photos of themselves. If they were flattered and agreed, he demanded even more photos and videos—this time in embarrassing and **inappropriate** poses. If a girl got upset and wanted to tell on him, he threatened to post her pictures online and ruin her life.

Sometimes, Gunn also fooled girls by pretending to be a new kid in town who just wanted to make friends. He created social media

Actor Russell Park portrayed North Korean dictator Kim Jong-un in the controversial film *The Interview*, which was pulled from general release after a hacking attack allegedly from North Korea.

Cyber criminals like Gunn take advantage of the love that many fans have for celebrities such as Justin Bieber to gather information or photographs from unsuspecting computer users.

profiles using various fake names. Once he had gained the trust of his victims, he asked them to reveal extremely personal information about themselves. Later, he demanded pictures of them undressed. If they refused, he threatened to email the personal information to their school principals or post it online for everyone to see.

Finally, a brave group of girls from one junior high school in Prattville, Alabama, got together. They told local police what was happening to them. When police realized that Gunn was preying on girls in several states, they contacted the FBI. The authorities were able to trace an IP address for one of the fake accounts back to Gunn's house, and they seized his computer. When they examined it, they found evidence of his scams, and Gunn is now serving a long prison sentence.

# Protect Yourself

Christopher Patrick Gunn was able to fool hundreds of girls into believing he was someone else. The cyber security experts at the social media site Facebook don't want you or their other 1.3 billion users to fall for anything like that.

People impersonate others for a variety of reasons—most of them bad. They may want to cyberbully someone without being held responsible, spread malware, trick people into something, or take advantage of them (such as Gunn did). They might also try a 419 scam—a type of fraud in which the potential victim is promised a share of a large sum of money in exchange for a favor. Sometimes, the impersonators try to shut down the real accounts of the people they are impersonating so that they seem more believable.

Facebook offers these tips so you can identify fake profiles and what you should be paying attention to. Similar methods work on other social media sites.

- If a friend or follower of someone you know wants to be your friend as well, it doesn't always mean your friend knows them in person. Even if you see you have mutual friends, learn more about the person before accepting the friend request.

- Is your friend posting items and sharing photos that seem out of character? Someone could be impersonating him or her!

- It is highly unlikely that a pop star or famous actor will simply contact you on a social media site.

- If you think someone is pretending to be someone they are not, report it to Facebook or whatever social site you're on. Members of their team will investigate. If the identity of the person can't be verified, the team will close the account. If they have reason to believe that the person is dangerous, they will contact a law-enforcement agency.

Selfies are forever; be careful what you post.

# An Un-merry Holiday Season

azio Mechanical Services, a company in Pennsylvania, installs and services refrigeration, heating, and air conditioning systems. One day at work, they were surprised to get a visit from the U.S. Secret Service. They were even more surprised when the agents began questioning them about credit card theft. None of them would ever think of stealing a credit card. One of them, however, had responded to a **phishing** email. Phishes are scams in which the recipient of the email is tricked into clicking on a phony Web site and revealing private information. A Fazio employee had given criminals the credentials to access the retail chain Target's computers using a phishing scam.

In late November 2013, the criminals uploaded malicious card-stealing software to a small number of cash registers within Target stores. By the end of the month, just in time for the Christmas shopping season, they had installed their malware on a majority of Target's point-of-sale devices. They were busily collecting credit and debit card numbers from customers.

By the middle of December, when the breach was discovered, about 40 million card numbers had been taken. Target security experts scrubbed the malware as soon as it was detected, but it was a little too late. Authorities believe that the stolen financial information was sent to thieves in the United States, Russia, and Brazil. It was a massive hack, and Target spent more than $60 million to fix it. *Bloomberg Business Week* called it "the biggest retail hack in U.S. history." The theft gave cyber security experts a look at a new kind of hack, however, so they can be on guard next time.

# A Coordinated Caper

*I*n 2008, a group of criminals pulled off a heist as carefully timed and choreographed as any ballet. Spread out around the globe, the thieves stole more than $9 million from some 2,000 ATM machines in the United States, Canada, Italy, Japan, Russia, and other countries—all within about 12 hours.

The **masterminds** were four hackers from Eastern Europe who learned about a **vulnerability** in the computer network of the Royal Bank of Scotland that was located in Atlanta, Ga. That system was connected to hundreds of others through its ATMs. The hackers got into the network and changed PINs (personal information numbers). Then they raised the limits on the amount of money that could be withdrawn from the accounts. The thieves made ATM cards tied to the new

ATMs are now used around the world, dispensing cash in the local currencies. Their connections to worldwide computer systems make them a target for cyber attack.

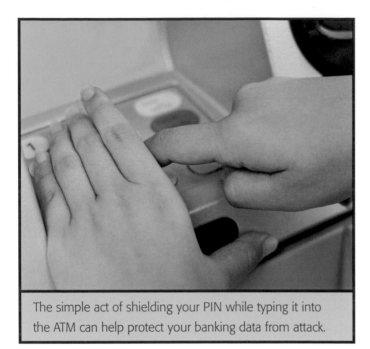

The simple act of shielding your PIN while typing it into the ATM can help protect your banking data from attack.

PINs and passed them out to accomplices. Thieves in countries around the world then used counterfeit cards at ATM machines.

The thieves—called "cashiers" in the **lingo** of the criminal world—fanned out at the same time. They hit local ATMs along planned routes. (In one small bit of poor planning, some cashiers who lived in the same city tried getting money from a machine, only to discover that a fellow cashier had gotten there earlier and emptied it.) As the cashiers worked, the masterminds monitored the computer network to keep track of their progress. They also made sure that the cashiers worked in a rolling series across time zones so that they hit at a time of day most likely to evade detection.

To the criminal gang's delight, withdrawal after withdrawal appeared in the records. Once the cashiers were done, the money was collected and divided up. Cashiers got a chunk. The rest went to the four hackers, who hadn't even left their houses.

Fortunately, the bank's security engineers discovered the breach right away. Federal authorities got to work. With the help of international agents, the hackers were caught and convicted. In one country in Europe, Estonia, the FBI provided information that led to the arrest of an entire string of the criminals and to the recovery of nearly $300,000.

Officials in the Netherlands and Hong Kong were also involved in finding the hackers. The thieves were arrested, though all the money was not recovered. As with many large cyber attacks, the key to foiling the scheme was international cooperation. Cyber attacks, unlike bank robbers, can't be stopped by border patrols or roadblocks.

Agents weren't surprised at the hackers' technical abilities. They had seen similar hacks. This case stood out because of the clockwork timing and the large group of cashiers. In the end, however, they still got caught by the people in the white hats.

# Text-Dependent Questions

1. What is the name of the device Matthew Weaver used to help him steal login information? What does it do?

2. Who did Christopher Patrick Gunn pretend to be?

3. In the criminal world, what is a cashier?

# Research Project

The FBI maintains a "Cyber Most Wanted" list. Look up the list online and find out what types of crimes were committed by the black-hat hackers. Did some steal credit card information? Did some try to find out U.S. military secrets?

# Scientists in the News

**4**

## George Hotz

When the iPhone was first released in 2007, people had to sign up with AT&T to use it. Seventeen-year-old George Hotz was a T-Mobile customer. He wanted an iPhone but did not want to switch companies. The solution? He opened the back of the phone with a tiny screwdriver. Then he used an electrical wire to scramble the code on one of its chips. Finally, he installed a program he had written himself. It enabled the iPhone to work for any wireless customer. Hotz became the first person ever to unlock an iPhone, an exploit that made headlines around the world. It was hard for many people to believe that a teenager could be that technologically adept!

Unlocking the phone wasn't illegal—Hotz says that he would never break the law—but Apple, the company that makes iPhones,

Hotz made headlines with his youthful discovery of a way around cell phones' security software.

was probably not very happy to have been hacked. Since then, Hotz has worked for big companies such as Google and Facebook, helping them discover and fix the bugs in their systems. If you are really, really smart, he says, maybe you could be a cyber security expert, too. "It doesn't matter how old you are, where you come from, the color of your skin, or whether you're male or female," he asserts. "Computers don't care. The Internet is the purest **meritocracy** ever built."

## Justin Cappos

Everyone knows by now that it's not a good idea to have a password that's easy to guess. (Yet the most popular password is…"password"!) Cappos, a professor of computer science and engineering at New York University, has a way to make passwords even safer. He has developed a password protection system so

Cappos' work has made millions of people's data safer by helping create better passwords.

### WORDS TO UNDERSTAND

**meritocracy**   a system in which skill and talent are the only reasons for advancement and success

efficient that all 900 million computers on Earth would need to cal-culate nonstop for longer than 13 billion years—the estimated age of the universe—to accomplish the same thing. For this work, Professor Cappos was named one of the most brilliant scientists in the world by *Popular Science* magazine.

His system works because it does not store each password's infor-mation individually, as most systems do. A would-be attacker would need to crack big groups of passwords simultaneously—an almost impossible task. Professor Cappos explains, "Imagine if you have 25 students in your class and you want to guess their birthdays one at a time. It wouldn't be all that hard because there are only 365 days in the year, and that means that you'd never have to make more than 365 guesses for each student before being correct. Now imagine that you have to guess all 25 birthdays correctly at the very same time. There are trillions and trillions of possible combinations, so you might have to make trillions and trillions of guesses in order to be right." The system, called PolyPasswordHasher, is open source. That means any business or organization can use it freely.

## Parisa Tabriz

Parisa Tabriz is the head of security for Google Chrome, but she thinks it's boring to call herself an Information Security Engineer. Instead, her business cards say "Security Princess."

The title may sound silly, but Tabriz has a serious job: to keep the popular Web browser safe from attacks. Tabriz also teaches Google's engineers how to think like hackers. She figures that if they know how Web sites are attacked, they'll know how to build strong defens-es by eliminating bugs in their code.

Tabriz didn't even own a computer until she was a student at the University of Illinois. When she wasn't in class studying computer engineering, she taught herself to build Web sites using a free service called Angelfire. Angelfire was free because its creators earned money by placing pop-up ads. As Tabriz worked, however, she did not want to read about new miracle drugs, vacation spots, or any of the other products that popped up on her screen. Using the skills she was learning in her computer engineering classes, she figured out a way to disable the ads. It was her first hack!

Only a few months after graduating from Illinois, Tabriz joined Google as a white-hat hacker. The Internet giant wanted her to make sure the company stayed a step ahead of the black hats. Now she makes sure no one can hack Google Chrome.

# Find Out More

## Books

Alexander, Tracy: *Hacked*. London: Piccadilly Press, 2014.
Note: This novel features a teenager involved with a cyber attack.

Ivester, Matt: *lol…OMG!: What Every Student Needs to Know About Online Reputation Management, Digital Citizenship, and Cyberbullying.* Serra Knight Publishing, 2012.

Sande, Warren and Carter Sandye Carter, *Hello World!: Computer Programming for Kids and Other Beginners.* Greenwich, Conn.: Manning Publications, 2013.

## Web Sites

www.carnegiecyberacademy.com/index.html
Visit the Carnegie Cyber Academy, where fun "training missions" teach how to spot spam, how to keep personal information private, and how to identify Web site traps such as forms that ask for personal information and Web pages that show inappropriate content.

www.nsa.gov/kids/
Learn about codes and ciphers, play fun games, and meet a cool cast of characters at this Web site brought to you by the National Security Agency.

www.facebook.com/safety
The Facebook Family Safety Center provides resources to ensure that kids, parents, and teachers are empowered to start conversations about online safety and know how to use Facebook tools.

# Series Glossary of Key Terms

**airlock**   a room on a space station from which astronauts can move from inside to outside the station and back

**anatomy**   a branch of knowledge that deals with the structure of organisms

**bionic**   to be assisted by mechanical movements

**carbon dioxide**   a gas that is in the air that we breathe out

**classified**   kept secret from all but a few people in a government or an organization

**deforestation**   the destruction of forest or woodland

**diagnose**   to recognize by signs and symptoms

**discipline**   in science, this means a particular field of study

**elite**   the part or group having the highest quality or importance

**genes**   information stored in cells that determine a person's physical characteristics

**geostationary**   remaining in the same place above the Earth during an orbit

**innovative**   groundbreaking, original

**inquisitiveness**   an ability to be curious, to continue asking questions to learn more

**internships**   jobs often done for free by people in the early stages of study for a career

**marine**   having to do with the ocean

**meteorologist**   a scientist who forecasts weather and weather patterns

**physicist**   a scientist who studies physics, which examines how matter and energy move and relate

**primate**   a type of four-limbed mammal with a developed brain; includes humans, apes, and monkeys

**traits**   a particular quality or personality belonging to a person

# Index

## Photo Credits

Dreamstime.com: Lyndale Woolcock 10; Ekzman 12; Leaf 18; Saniphoto 22; Verkoka 24; Balefire9 30; AMZphoto 36; Lianem 39; A. Singkham 40.

U.S. Army/Sgt. Kimberly Hackbarth, 6; Department of Defense/P.O. Jeremy Wood, 8; FBI: 14; Rose State College: 17; Nate Grigg: 19; Department of Homeland Security: 27; Shutterstock/Raw Pixel: 32; Newscom/UPI/Jim Raymen: 35; Newscom/The Record/Chris Pedota: 42; NYU Polytechnic School of Engineering: 43.

Scientists in Action logo by Comicraft.

## About the Author

Mari Rich was educated at Lehman College, part of the public City University of New York. As a writer and editor, she has had many years of experience in the fields of university communications and reference publishing, most notably with the highly regarded periodical *Current Biography*, aimed at high school and college readers. She also edited and wrote for *World Authors, Leaders of the Information Age,* and *Nobel Laureates.* Currently, she spends much of her time writing about engineers and engineering.